DEDICATION

This publication is dedicated to the women who have refused to give up their platforms, refused to bow to religiosity and instead, occupy their platforms...from motherhood to ministry, and beyond. *Thank you.*

CONTENTS

PUBLISHER'S NOTE

"John MacArthur to women:
  "Go home."

Jesus to women standing outside of His empty tomb:
  "Go and tell."

Let the Bible do the talking. Women change the world."[1]

Prior to curating this devotional, we came across an image that contained the quote above. The contrast is striking. When these controversial, careless words were uttered by a renowned leader, we decided to use our resources to make something happen. When we set out to do so, we carefully considered a course of action.

This book is by no means a rebuke, a correction, or a vengeful collective of quarrelsome teaching. The last thing needed is ad hominem attacks or a doctrinal stand-off.

Instead, we put together a simple compilation of encouragement, written *by* women *for* women.

A few have expressed uneasy sentiments toward the project title *Not Going Home;* such as, "Are you saying that women shouldn't focus on their role in the home?" or "Does this mean the contributors are refusing to acknowledge the value of their position in the home?" Emphatically, *no.*

The phrase and the movement **#notgoinghome** is a responsive statement that means, "I refuse to give up my ministry role because of my gender." It means, "I refuse to abandon my post as a communicator of the gospel because I am a woman."

To reduce women to *one* role is to suppress abilities that Christ wants to activate. This devotional is comprised of work from women from all over the U.S. and abroad. They are wives, CEO's, pastors, daughters, evangelists, business owners, stay-at-home moms, teachers, grandmothers, homemakers, and leaders.

Draw from their insight, experience, and wisdom as you receive lasting encouragement to stay the course and maximize your influence as a called and ordained *woman of God.*

1

MADE FOR MORE

BY MRS. BRYNN LEIGH SHAMP

THERE IS A GOD WHISPER THAT CALLS OUT TO YOUR SOUL; stretching across time and space, reverberating in the halls of destiny, echoing your name. He calls to you. The Great One. The Creator. The One who was and is and is to come. He calls you by name. He separates the cosmos and peals back the terrestrial canopy to gaze upon your very existence. He is the one they call Emmanuel. He is the God with us. So if he is the God with us, he can never be the God without us. He has forever forged his Divine Spirit in union with the spirit of humanity and declares, "You were made for more!"

You dust of the Earth that I formed and fashioned with my very own hands. You that I breathed the very atmosphere of Heaven into your lungs. You that I crowned with authority and dominion. You are forever mine. You have captured my heart, and I will not let go.

This is how the Father, God, sees you. You may not see yourself in the same exact light, but if we take a moment to remember what the Scripture says we will find that He knew us even before we were formed in our Mother's womb.

> "Oh yes, you shaped me first inside, then out; you formed me in my mother's womb. I thank you, High God—you're breathtaking! Body and soul, I am marvelously made! I worship in adoration—what a creation! You know me inside and out, you know every bone in my body; You know exactly how I was made, bit by bit, how I was sculpted from nothing into something. Like an open book, you watched me grow from conception to birth; all the stages of my life were spread out before you, The days of my life all prepared before I'd even lived one day." (Psalm 139: 13-16, MSG)

He knows you. He loves you. He moved Heaven and Earth to reach you. No matter the current circumstance or situation you find yourself in today, He is closer than a breath away. Through Christ Jesus, you have been given empowerment to reign in this life. You have been fashioned with the precise skill set and unique personality to accomplish God's divine destiny for your life. He did not give you a voice to remain silent. In fact, Psalm 68:11(NIV) declares, "The Lord announces the word, and the women who proclaim it are a mighty throng:"

You belong to a company of women who know their Father and know their worth!

—MRS. BRYNN LEIGH SHAMP
DESTINY ENCOUNTERS INTL. |
MORAVIAN FALLS, NORTH CAROLINA

MARY, DID YOU REALLY KNOW?

BY PAIGE SAGACH

I WONDER...

Mary, did you really know how one angel's visit would radically change your life for ever?

Did you know that your very life would be on the line because of your decision?

Did you know that the king of your country would seek to murder your innocent newborn baby?

Did you know that you would have to live in a foreign country to keep your baby alive?

Did you know that you would have to watch your son be praised and ridiculed at the same time?

Did you know that you would have to watch your precious son die young?

Did you know that your very name would live on throughout history?

Did you know that you were chosen out of all the young women in the world to bring forth the most important message to mankind?

Did you know that your decision would effect future generations to come?

One more question…

Mary, did you really know what you were doing when you said, "I am the Lord's servant. May everything you have said about me come true"?

I cannot imagine that Mary knew all that she was destined for, not even a little bit. But I do know that she made a decision that her faith in God would be bigger than her fears.

She wasn't perfect. She was just a girl. But she was willing to say "Yes" to her God.

Now It's your turn…

Do you know all that God has destined for you?

Do you know that He has chosen you out of all the women in the world to fulfill a mission that is specific to you?

Do you know that it is going to be difficult at times?

Do you know that people might ridicule you and laugh at you?

Do you know that it will be the most rewarding and fulfilling thing you've ever done?

Do you know that your decision will affect generations to come?

Oh, one more question.

Are you going to say "no" to God's plan for your life because you're too scared or you don't think you are capable, or are you going to let your faith in God crush your fears?

I pray your answer will be...

"I am the Lord's servant. May everything you have said about me come true." (Luke 1:38)

—Paige Sagach
New Life Bristol | Bristol, Indiana

RELENTLESS

BY ROCHELLE STECH

ENDURANCE. EXPECTATION. FAITH. THESE THINGS HAVE BEEN rolling through my heart lately and I want to encourage you, dear one, to keep going, expecting and believing. When the going gets rough and different seasons in life come where "one day at a time" is your reality as you're believing God, consider Romans 5:3-5. The passage encourages and enlightens us that the things we go through in life teach us patience, will give us experience and produce expectation.

As we start seeing the faithfulness of God come through in our situation(s); and as we experience God's love and favor, the fears begin to turn into faith and doubts turn into expectation. The Scripture encourages us in Romans 5:5 that as we put our expectation in God, He will never bring us shame or disappointment.

Recently, I was reading out of Genesis 32:24-32 and it spoke of Jacob wrestling with the angel of the Lord from evening until day break the next morning. Though the struggle continued long, Jacob kept his ground and his faith was not shaken, nor did he silence his prayer. He wanted a blessing! The angel of the Lord even disabled Jacob's hip as a reminder that Jacob must no longer walk in his own strength but must rely entirely on God. Although Jacob's hip was out of socket he kept wrestling – he wouldn't relent until he was blessed.

Jacobs desire for God's blessing on his life, the fervent-ness of his persistency that night - even with a hip out of socket, and his faith in getting that blessing, greatly spoke to me. Zechariah 4:6 says, "It's not by our strength or our power but by my Spirit, says the Lord of hosts". Victory and blessing in our lives come the same way. While we may not actually wrestle physically with God, we can seek Him persistently and seriously in prayer with the expectation of end results.

Jacob's story encouraged me to endure during the waiting and not lose patience; to trust God and His promises no matter how long it takes. His expectation in God chal-lenged me to not take no for an answer - even if things seem to get worse before they get better. His faith propelled me to have relentless trust and assurance in the God that answered his prayers.

I pray that this touched your heart today. Know God is for you and loves you. He believes in you. His word is a lamp unto our feet and a light unto our paths. May your world be lit up by revelation, power, and direction as you pour the word of God into your hearts and minds.

—ROCHELLE STECH
NEW LIFE BRISTOL | BRISTOL, INDIANA

4

BEFORE YOU ASK

BY DIANA PRICE

"Therefore do not be like them. For your Father knows the things you have need of before you ask Him." (Matthew 6:8)

MY HUSBAND AND I HAD JUST MADE A QUICK TRIP TO TN AND back. It's a long 8 hour drive but this trip it turned into 10 hours due to traffic delays. I had lots of time to think about the drive and it reminded me of our relationship.

As we drove along we encountered many moments of irritation because of delays. There were stinky moments when we drove past a farm or the scent of a skunk tinged the air. There were hangry moments, corrected with a snack. Then came the loud music, crazy fun dancing moments when the best song came over the radio. But for most part the drive was spent sitting quietly and just being in each other's presence. Those are the best moments.

In my husband's presence, I know that if we break down he's more than capable of getting us back on the road. If we need gas, he won't wait until we're traveling on fumes to pull over. Or If I'm simply just hungry, I only need to say so and he quickly responds to my needs. At times, he's already deciding to pull over because he knows I will need to use the restroom soon.

I have an amazing husband.

But y'all, did you know that's exactly the relationship we have with God? This is what He desires? Your presence. Those sitting quietly and just being together moments. Through the delays, the irritations, the crazy fun dancing moments, and the stinky times- ALL of it: He just wants to be there in your presence. And if you remain in His presence, he will take care of all your needs.

With God; I know that if I break down, I'm taken care of. If I need strength, he's got it covered. If I need something, I just need to say so. My wants and needs are taken care of, graciously. I have an even more amazing God.

I remember going through a rough season in my life.My husband and I had raised four boys that were now all men and not making the best choices. We prayed for release from drugs, alcohol, and behaviors that pulled them further from Christ. One of our sons was looking at prison time. To top it of, we had 3 grandchildren arrive overnight to live with us because their home life wasn't great. In that season (which was years in length) we felt attacked on all sides.

One day at the beginning of this season, we had acquired a minivan. It was cheap and so we thought why not? We could just flip it and make some extra cash. Two days later the grandkids came to live with us. Our God knew our needs before we did!

As this season progressed and it was heavier and heavier,

and I became more and more overwhelmed; my prayers were this- "Father I thank You for guiding me and holding me. I don't understand why this is all happening but I know that You're In control. For that alone I'm very grateful. My Spirit feels You but my flesh needs a physical and tangible sign that You're moving. Could you do that for me please?"

The next day an unexpected check for $5,000.00 showed up. Wow!

When you know who your Father is. When you just remain in His presence. You are taken care of. He knows your needs before you do.

—Diana Price
New Life Christian Church | Milford, Indiana

WHO ARE YOU?

BY AMANDA EASON

"Write also concerning the Jews as it pleases you in the king's name, and seal it with the king's [signet] ring-for writing which is in the king's name & sealed with the king's ring no man can reverse." (Esther 8:8)

THE KING'S RULE HELD GREAT AUTHORITY DURING ANCIENT times. So much so that once a statement from the king had been sealed, showing it to be valid & authentic, no man could reverse it. Esther 8:8 tells us that Queen Esther had found such favor in the king's sight that he allowed her complete use of his name, with all of the power & authority that accompanied it.

Our Father, the King of Kings, has given us this same use of His name today, along with all the power & authority that accompanies it. When we use the name of Jesus when we pray or when we declare His Word over our lives, it isn't something we should take lightly. The name of Jesus is powerful & holds great authority. Just as the king trusted

Queen Esther with use of his name, our King, Jesus has done the same.

In your prayer time this week ask God to give you a deeper revelation of the name of Jesus and all of the power and benefits that the use of that name holds. Ephesians 1:17 tells us to ask God for the spirit of wisdom and revelation so that we can gain insight into a deeper understanding of who He is. This is the name that Peter used in Acts 3:6 when he said to the lame beggar, "Silver or gold I do not have, but what I do have I give you, in the Name of Jesus Christ of Nazareth, walk." What Peter had was revelation of the Name of Jesus, of the authority and power that it held and the understanding that he had the right to use it.

As women in today's society we have many voices telling us who we "are" or who we should be, but there is only ONE voice that matters. That voice is the voice of our heavenly Father. He tells us we are royalty who walks in the authority of His Name, we are CALLED to make His name famous, and most of all we are HIS.

—Amanda Eason
Grace Through the Fire Ministries | Wilson, North
Carolina

EVEN IN THIS

BY KATIE CLAMPIT

WE ALL HAVE THEM. THOSE SITUATIONS THAT MAKE US FEEL like our heart is being ripped out. The situation there is no solution to right now. The one you want so badly to fix, but there is not anything you can do about it.

You already have it in your head, don't you?

A few weeks ago, I was driving to Atlanta and I was talking to Jesus. I had been dealing with one of those situations, and I was feeling really discouraged. I was asking God to intervene and crying out again. Asking Him why we had to keep going around this circle over and over. Trying to reconcile in my mind why He won't just fix it.

But as always – He is teaching me to trust Him just a little deeper.

I was playing my worship music and going on my soapbox, when He asked me this:

"Katie, won't you trust me...even in this?"

It was the last 3 words that broke me down. The "even in this" – because I realized that still I was putting boundaries on my trust. I was still trying to control this one thing. I was still trying to fix it so I wouldn't have to be afraid. I was still trying to maintain a little control, and that isn't what He's asking of me.

God was asking me to allow Him to tear down another wall. To rip apart another lie. He was asking me to not allow fear to creep in because His love is the cure.

Here's the deal: You don't have to know what is coming. You don't have to know the solution to the problem. You don't have to know how it all works out. All you have to know is that Jesus is already there. He's always been there. There is security in that. There is safety in that. There is peace in that.

There is a song called "You Came" by Jonathan David and Melissa Hesler. It's one of my favorite songs because it says, "You came…. I knew that you would come."

I tear up every time I hear the line, "I knew that you would come."

I don't know the solution to your situation. I don't know how God is going to intervene or what brave steps He will guide you to take.

But what I do know is:

Even in this, you can trust that He will come. He always comes. And when Jesus shows up – things change.

Friends be encouraged. He is good. He is patient. He is pursuing you. He is kind and He can be trusted…even in this.

—Katie Clampit
Oak City Church | Birmingham, Alabama

KNOWN BY CHRIST

BY DIONNE HITSON

In Luke 13:22-27, Jesus makes it clear that He wants relationship not religion. Neither does He want traditions of man, lip service, or going through the motions. We each must have a personal relationship with Him in order to be recognized as His own. We cannot oppose the LORD or His word, or make excuses for not obeying His word. The LORD wants our heart. He wants our commitment and our willingness to make any sacrifice that He will ask us to make, to include trusting Him no matter the cost, no matter how it looks, or no matter how it feels (2 Corinthians 5:7, Hebrews 11:6).

The LORD wants us to have a "ride or die" attitude and commitment toward Him even during the times we fall. When we fall we can't quit and give up. We have to repent and keep going like David did (Psalm 51). Relationship, trust, and obedience are the only ways of entering the Kingdom of God, there are no other ways (John 10:1-2). Though many have come in the past and will come in the future; and say there are other ways of entering the Kingdom of God, those ways only lead to the path of deception, death, and eternity in hell (1 Timothy 4:1).

Yes, hell is real. Yes, we can send ourselves there by deceiving ourselves into believing we can do what we want, live how we want, and spend eternity in heaven with the LORD. The LORD is Holy and can't look upon sin. Look at Lucifer, he had pride in his heart that led him to the desire to be like God, the creator of heaven and earth, thus he was kicked out of heaven as fast as a lightning (Isaiah 14:14, Genesis 1:1, Luke 10:18). Now is not the time to play around with our soul and take the risk of not spending eternity with God in heaven. Once our spirits leave this earth, it'll be too late to decide to have a personal relationship with the LORD, unless He performs a supernatural miracle in you and raises you from the dead and brings you back to the earth to get it right with Him. But why take that risk? To be known by Christ is to live for Christ. Selah.

—DIONNE HITSON
CONSUMING FIRE CHRISTIAN CENTER | WESTLAND, MICHIGAN

RECONCILE: THE WAY

BY ALLY PINNOCK

HER BROKENNESS LOOKED BEAUTIFUL TO HIM...

He only saw perfection, but wounded from rejection she hid under a heavy cloak of shame.

Able to see from The Heart He knew she'd been set apart so he pursued her like a dart for she was to him a work of art...

She:

She kept her distance.

He was persistence personified.

Poisoned by past pains, she built a brick building around her shame cloaked soul hoping nobody would see.

She:

Angered by wounds from wars with words, ways which were once accepted that had been directed right at her petal lovely heart, hovering in the dark of her empty stolen being.

He:

Set the girl alight with a bright flight of feathers he'd

been saving just for her, for he knew her from before the foundations of the world. He'd formed her innermost being.

He:

Seeing all and being all he knew about the fall and so did she.

The way had come to her doorstep. Rapping on her dark heavy locked door with such tender mercy that it sparked a kindle of hope in the darkness of her scars and so she let him in.

Come in beloved she heard her lips release a whisper and all of a sudden: Peace was present in this place. Tears fell down her face for this amazing grace had finally set her free.

She:

Falling to her knees placing kisses on his feet, heart open, darkness broken, soul awoken. The Word had spoken.

They:

United as one.

Eternity begun.

Both a Son of the Holy One.

God had won.

—Ally Pinnock
The Academy of Creative Transformation |
Sydney, Australia

THE JOURNEY OF HOPE

BY ANNE B SAY

"Now these three remain: faith, hope, and love. But the greatest of these is love. Pursue love..." (1 Corinthians 13:13-14:1)

- Why these things?
- Where do we come off the path?
- How does this progression happen?

IN THIS LETTER PAUL WAS WRITING TO A YOUNG CHURCH THAT was struggling with division, morality, idolatry, and theology. This young church with these troubles could easily exist today.

The journey of hope begins in faith. Remember, faith is an action word, not a noun. It's not a thing. It's an action a believer takes because she trusts in God, in His word, in His promises. From the very beginning of our coming to Jesus, we act in faith.

The journey of hope begins with an act of faith, a decision to embark on a journey. This journey has a path and a destination. Consider a train station and the tracks the train travels on.

Faith gets us to the train station. The decision to follow Jesus is the action to start the journey. Hope is the train tracks.

Hope is what keeps us on the journey. We believe all the promises God speaks over us. Hope keeps us waiting expectantly while we're on the journey.

But life happens. There is an enemy who wants nothing more than to derail our journey. Why? Because our destination is Love. Love has a name, and His name is Jesus. The journey of hope is the journey of staying strong in the storms so that we don't get derailed and fall short of our destination.

Two things derail us. Fear and shiny objects. Fear derails us one side because when we take our eyes off Love, Jesus, we think, like Peter walking on the water, that we're going to die. Shiny objects, money, fame, nice things derail us the other side Because we take our eyes off Jesus and pursue these things with more passion than pursuing Him, Love.

Faith gets us on the journey. Hope keeps us going. Love is our destination, and love is a relationship.

The destination is both where we are headed and the fuel that keeps us going.

The journey of faith is the journey of staying in relationship with Love, Jesus, so that we don't get derailed by things like fear and shiny objects.

We stay on the journey when we remember who we are. Redeemed, A daughter of the King, Beloved. Love is reminding us continuously who we are. And Love reminds us of who He is for us. The Fuel for our journey, our Comforter, our Guide, our Resource for everything we need in life.

Faith and hope meet life, and Love reminds us who we are and who He is for us.

We always have enough faith. We always have hope. The thing we always need to watch is how Love is working in and through us to keep us on the destination to His heart.

It's about progress, not perfection, on the journey.

—Anna B Say
Atlanta, Georgia

A WOMAN'S GLORY

BY SHANA DORSEY

"Woman is the glory of man." (1 Corinthians 11:7 NIV)

IN OUR DAY AND AGE, THERE'S MUCH INSECURITY AROUND US women. It seems we must prove that we are just as smart, capable and strong as men; but we already know that we are just as worthy as men—right?

Subjectively, in our own hearts, the answer may vary depending on our moods and cultural norms. But objectively, the answer is in Genesis. God made Adam first and out of his rib he fashioned Eve (Genesis 2:23). Though Adam was made first, it did not alter the woman's worth.

The woman was very much a reflection of Adam's body and nature. She was another human being yet wholly "other" from him. The softness of the woman's body, the arch of her curves, length of her hair –were all very much indicators of her "otherness" from him. Yet with her two legs, two arms, torso, eyes , ears, nose and mouth, she was unmistakably like him. She was a reflection of Adam but also her own person, with a distinct identity from him.

The scriptures affirm her worth stating, "So God created mankind in his own image, in the image of God he created them; male and female he created them." (Genesis 1:27)

God's word clearly states that "mankind" is two-part and each part equally contributes to "mankind". So, as women, we are a part of the one race of "man". We are very much equal in dignity to men and in fact together with men reveal the nature of God. Here's how.

God uses gender in a man and woman to reflect the utter separation in personhood that is in the Father and the Son. As a man and a woman can come together as one being in marriage, the Son and the Father are both distinct individuals but also are one God (John 14:11).

In addition, the order of submission and authority that God has ordained in marriage between man and woman, finds its origins in God's relationship with himself. The Father corresponds to Man, while the Son corresponds to the Woman. Eve was hidden in Adam's side, then taken out to marry him. Likewise, Christ dwells hidden in the "bosom" of the Father (John 1:18), proceeds from the Father and in maturity submits in loving return to the Father. "But I want you to realize that the head of every man is Christ, and the head of the woman is man, and the head of Christ is God." (1 Corinthians 11:3, NIV). In God's unique plan for man and woman, we see God's own unity in diversity.

As women, we have the beautiful privilege of illustrating Christ's role before the Father. Our worth comes not from men, what we do or even from ourselves. Our worth comes from the fact that we were created in the image of God, alongside men: and as women, we uniquely show forth the beauty of God's Son.

—Shana Dorsey
Shana Dorsey Ministries | Jacksonville, Florida

A PERSONAL TESTIMONY

BY WENDY HIBBARD

IT WAS OUR FIRST DATE. WHEN HE ASKED ME TO MEET HIM AT A fancy golf club for dinner, my interest peaked. It was the same club where my father had worked as a boy. I'd never been there before, and the thought of connecting with a piece of my father's past made my heart happy. This was going to be fun! Or so I thought.

Somehow, in all of his stories, my father never once mentioned it was a "Men Only" club. He (my date) was welcome to stay, but I was not. The evening never recovered.

Fast forward to a couple years ago, when a friend asked me to accompany her to a nearby church. They were in the process of presbytery elections, and several candidates were being introduced. A mix of men and women, each candidate was seated next to their spouse on the platform.

As introductions proceeded, the male applicants were lavished with praise and admiration. When it came to the female applicants, impressive resumes each? Well, that was a different story.

Their accomplishments were listed, immediately followed by jokes about how much trouble they cause their husbands, or how it would have been impossible for them to accomplish any of these impressive feats without Bill, or David, or Jackson. Then the conversation quickly shifted to Bill, or David or Jackson, where it remained for the rest of the introduction.

It was astounding. And so incredibly demeaning. There were no signs posted, no official policies. Yet this too, in many ways, was a "Men Only" club. It caught me off guard, considering it was a satellite church beneath a senior leader I respect. I don't believe he would have signed off on such disrespectful treatment of women who'd made applications to serve his church. But, there's a little leaven amidst a lot of leadership teams. And in some cases, the leaven is practically all that's left.

When I first got saved, I was bombarded with books by a popular theologian and ministry leader. Much of my early foundation came from those works. Unbeknownst to me, or the female pastor who'd first recommended them, he was solidly opposed to women in ministry, or any kind of leadership role.

That was a long time ago. Frankly, I'd forgotten about it until recently. When a series of derogatory statements against women in ministry from the same leader surfaced, I was shocked. Bias against women in ministry is not new. But I was having a personal reaction. It felt like I'd been slapped and formally disinherited by...a father?

And it really hurt. I wasn't prepared for that. But my heavenly Father was. He cloaked me in the consuming fire of his love. Those hidden lies of limitation? Up in smoke.

I no longer take abuse from spiritual fathers lightly. I am, first and foremost, a daughter of the Most High God. And I refuse to relinquish my birthright, my inheritance, or the call of God upon my life.

—WENDY HIBBARD
GLOBAL FIRE CHURCH | NASHVILLE, TENNESSEE

WE ARE DAUGHTERS

BY JENNIFER NEWELL

AS WE CROSS INTO THIS NEW SEASON, IT'S VERY EASY TO SEE that the topic of women in ministry and where we belong, is at a boiling point once again. We have made much progress, yet much more lays before us. It may occasionally feel as if the glass ceiling is going to crash down on our heads in the presence of our brethren. Some seek to find a champion in this hour, a person of influence who can quell the negativity that has been given a spotlight. However, we already have the only hero we'll ever need.

We are not damsels in distress, nor are we lesser citizens in this Kingdom. We are daughters of the Most High God, and He fights for us! Our most excellent calling is to rest in the identity of His beloved child. To be known as His daughters and called as His own, should be the sincerest desire of our hearts. Yes, we are mothers, wives, sisters, and warriors. But above all things, we are daughters!

We will never be denied by The One who created us and placed His gifts inside us. He prepares a table before us in the presence of our enemies, and He prepares a way for us in which to walk. He hides us in the shadow of His wings, and He will make our faces to shine like the noon day sun. We have been created for such a time as this, and we'll do it as daughters with all the rights and privileges of Kingdom heiresses, bestowed by our Heavenly Father. The scepter of grace has been extended to us, walk worthy.

—Jennifer Newell
Gateway Harvest House | Lenoir, North Carolina

13

REBUILDING

BY BONNIE DILLASHAW

MANY OF US ARE TIRED OF COMPLACENCY AND WATERED DOWN truth. We are starving for the real, authentic glory of God. We see the need for unity like never before and are willing to sacrifice our own comfort to honor one another and see His Bride awaken. There is a mandate to rebuild that drives us!

We have been commissioned by the King to raise His standard, to go in and take back our land.

Now is the time to rebuild the wall just as in the days of Nehemiah.

We are a generation walking out of places of bondage and into a land of promise. This land of promise currently lies desolate and in ruins. It's hard to see the boundaries of truth that once were. This promised land needs justice, it needs truth and protection.

We have Holy Spirit vision and are willing to overcome the obstacles that make our destiny appear impossible. These obstacles are trying to keep us from moving forward, from hearing direction, and from tasting His goodness!

The enemy has seen our ambition and tenacity. He has been using tactics to distract us and cause us to question everything. This retaliation of the enemy is because we are light; We are exposing and uncovering the wickedness that wants to call what is Holy, evil, and evil, Holy.

The tactics of the enemy in this hour are:

- Mockery/Accusation
- Confusion
- Intimidation
- Oppression
- Conspiracy

"Nevertheless, we made our prayer to our God, and because of them we set a watch against them day and night." (Nehemiah 4:9)

The Lord has given us keys to overcome:

- Prayer/Intercession!
- Set a watch by day and night!
- Holy Spirit is your watchman, your rear guard.
- Press into Holy Spirit and walk with Him daily.

Tune your ears to His voice, taking every thought captive. If the voice produces fear and confusion, it is not the Lord. Cast it away, keeping your hand to the plow. Don't look back.

Bind your mind to truth, the Word of God. Be careful of compromise. Choose purity! Compromise will be a trap. Take up arms (Full Armor), and praise Him, your worship is your weapon. Remember! Remembering that the Lord is Great and Awesome!

"Do not be afraid of them. Remember the Lord, great and awesome, and fight for your brethren, your sons, your daughters." (Nehemiah 4:14)

Invite the Fear of The Lord to walk with you!

"Should you not walk in the fear of our God because of the reproach of the nations, our enemies?" (Nehemiah 5:9)

Use the tactics of the enemy to propel you onward, knowing that this retaliation is only because you are taking ground. For every attack, the wall of truth and protection is going higher.

Do not be discouraged, do not be dismayed.

We are building upon a solid foundation, the walls that will house the Glory of the Lord.

We will not be silent, we will not stop, we are building the New Jerusalem.

—Bonnie Dillashaw
The Church at WarHill | Clermont, Georgia

14

LOVE WORTH LIVING FOR

BY HEATHER SCHULTZ

"What's wrong with me, Lord?" I asked with tear-stained eyes. The morning sun enveloped me with its warmth while the March winds encouraged a melody from the wind-chime hanging above me. I was sitting in my sweet spot on the back porch - the place where I can pour out my heart to God alone.

"It just seems that friends come and go. Very few stay in my life long. Is it me? Is there something wrong with me?" I prayed.

I could sense the Lord comforting me with the gentle reminder that He loves me. He approves of me.

I stood up, wiped my eyes, and whispered, "You'll be fine, Heather. Trust in the Lord. It's His opinion of you that matters the most anyway."

As I headed back indoors, I couldn't help but wonder how many people ask the same question. The message in our current society says, "Don't worry about what other people think. Just be you." Yet, when we try to be ourselves, the world turns against us. We offend others. We appear different. We think uniquely. We're turned away when we don't measure up; and when we do somehow measure up, we're looked down upon out of jealousy or envy. I mean, is it really okay to just be me?

After 40 years of trying to gain approval from others but being rejected time and again, I've finally resorted to the fact that seeking love from the world is just fickle. It's conditional. If we try to earn our way into being accepted by others and believe that our value is determined by that acceptance, then we have been greatly deceived.

Our value comes only from Jesus. Without Him, we are nothing. So, why do we continue to strive for love from others when His love is the only love that satisfies? In the end, it will not matter if we gained popularity. It will not matter if we had 10,000 social media followers or ten. What will matter is if we believed God at His word.

When the world was against us, we still chose to believe. We didn't allow the rejection of the world to define us. We didn't allow the lies of our enemies to tear us down. Instead, we stood in Truth. We believed that through it all, we would overcome because of Christ.

We believed that, "We are more than conquerors through Him who loved us," (Romans 8:37) because nothing in this world could ever separate us from the love of God. (Romans 8:38-39) Nothing. Nobody.

If you're in a place where you feel like the world is against you, you feel alone, you feel unloved or devalued, know this: You are loved. You are approved by the Creator of the Universe because of Jesus! When others don't see your worth, just remember that He thought you were worth dying for. Now, that's love worth living for!

—HEATHER SCHULTZ
HEATHER SCHULTZ MINISTRIES | TYLER, TEXAS

15

MAKING THINGS WHOLE AGAIN

BY LISA HELBLING FORD

RECENTLY, I DECIDED TO BAKE BREAD. IT HAD BEEN AWHILE since I baked, so I had to search my cabinets for a loaf pan. As I peered into the cabinet my eyes darted to an indigo blue speckled stone loaf pan stuck in the far back corner. Although the pan was gifted to me in 1984 today was the first time I ever considered using it. It was purchased in 1984 by my friend's mom, Mrs. Oudt, as a wedding gift intended for my June wedding.

Well, Mrs. Oudt made it to the wedding but, the gift was left behind. After that, over the years, I would see her and she would always tell me that she had my wedding gift wrapped in her closet. Then in 2010, her daughter, my old friend Juls, came to visit her mom and invited some old friends over to reconnect. I was shocked when her mom walked in the room with my 26 year old wrapped wedding present. We laughed and joked about it all night but, I honestly don't remember what was said. I'm sure my mouth dropped open and I may have seemed ungrateful. I could only think about the irony of the situation since my marriage of 26 years had ended just months before. There is no way she could have known. It was a big unexpected shock to everyone including myself. I opened the box and thought about throwing the stone pan to the ground. Then, like my heart, it would be in hundreds of pieces.

Instead, I thought of Mrs. Oudt and how she had saved it all those years. So I kept it, never intending to use it. I opened a kitchen cabinet and stuck it the far back corner and went on with my messed up life. But today, 34 years after it was purchased and 8 years after I stuffed it away, I used it for the first time to bake my bread. And I used it joyfully remembering my friends and thanking God for the lessons I have learned and new found peace and happiness He has blessed me with. I'm not without sad moments and completely over what happened but, I am consistently feeling better than ever and am not as overwhelmed with life. Have you ever fought so hard to hold on to something that you completely lost yourself in the process?

It's a crazy day when God speaks to your heart through His word and tells you to end something that you had been fighting for like crazy. To finally let go and walk away from a situation that has been controlled completely by your will to keep it going. And then to see the very worst possible things occur when you do so. To feel helpless and alone because the people around you can't handle your pain and feel like they don't know you anymore. That is what happened when my marriage ended. I had worked so hard, for so many years, to keep my family together. All I had feared and worse happened and I could not stop it. Days of pain turned into years of pain. But in the midst of that pain, God never left me and He provided the grace I desperately needed . I have learned that pain can bring healing when we are willing to forgive and let go. God has showed me the value of living honestly and the true freedom that it produces.

Many days my pain was accompanied by happiness and the adventure of living a new life. I have learned it is possible for pain and joy to coexist at the same moment of an entire day. In the past 8 years I have come to know God in a different and deeper way. He is authentic, honest and a truth lover. He cares more about me than I could ever have imagined. He is a courage giver, protector, healer and a friend. He is majestic and all of His creation is beautiful and full of passion. It makes me sad that He is unknown, misunderstood and misrepresented by many of His human creations. I write all of this to testify that God is real and worth knowing! He is not a figment of imagination or a dreamed up religion. Jesus is the essence of everything that is love. His spirit is looking to partner with you for life and eternity. My heart longs for all to embrace Jesus. I will live out the rest of my life with unhindered hope in all that He is. And I know that I am hidden and protected in His love. He has restored my life and given me what I needed most - His love. (Isaiah 54)

—LISA HELBING FORD
THATHEWOULDBEKNOWN.COM | DALLAS, GEORGIA

16

YOU ARE HOME

BY MARY LACY

From the moment that God created the concept of a woman, He established the place and belonging for her significance: In His Love, In His authority, In His plan. With no other rival in His determination of creation, WOMAN was an original thought with a significant purpose. As a woman, YOU were an INTENTION of God's heart to bring something specifically unique to this world that was lacking. When God was continuing His creation process, He never asked Adam's permission to continue His creative work. God saw the significance of creating woman to bring a dynamic that Adam alone did not have. Not less than or underneath, not more than or superior, but a CO-PARTNER with what He was doing in the world.

"So God created man in His own image; in the image of God He created him; male and female He created them. God blessed them and said to them, "Be fruitful and multiply, and fill the earth and subdue it; rule over the fish of the sea and the birds of the air and every creature that crawls upon the earth." (Genesis 1:27, 28)

When God created FEMALE, did He confine her and say – "In THIS place you belong, but no other?" No. In fact He addressed both men and women TOGETHER, never separating woman from the man. God spoke to them both – Go OUT into the world, be fruitful, multiply and have authority and dominion over everything I have placed under your feet as CO-LABORERS. The Father needs both man AND woman to bring His heart and purpose into this world. When man (Adam) saw the completion of God's creation, he welcomed and celebrated it. But if Adam had been AFRAID of the strength in the woman, God's co-laboring plan would not have worked. Only a man living in his own fear would reject the woman of partnership and strength...

God impregnated women with the miraculous ability to hold and birth LIFE. You, as the woman, are a LIFE-GIVER. Just as God the Father swooped her into Adam's world to make his life better, a woman that walks with her Creator has the ability inside of her to come into any situation and make things better. Your DNA presence as a woman carries the ability to create and bring life – in your home, in your workplace, in your schools, in your relationships, in your VOICE.

As we see how God established the significance of a woman, there is no doubt that women were not created to be sent away, to be shut down. God was not creating woman to be turned away. Quite the contrary, because WOMAN is so significant in His purposes, God was establishing that with HIM you already ARE home. "Home" is a symbolism of a place of belonging, safety, purpose, and rest. You are home by belonging with God and co-laboring with man. You are home in belonging in this world - to partner with God in His purposes. And your female presence has the capability of bringing the sense of "home" to others WHEREVER you go.

You, my dear, bring color to this world. You were not meant to be confined. You were meant to be celebrated... With God, you ARE home.

—Mary Lacy
Life Unscripted | San Diego, California

17

YOUR BODY IS GOOD: THE INCARNATION AS A CALL TO EMBODIMENT

BY SARA ROBBERT

OUR BODIES ARE A BEAUTIFUL DISPLAY OF GOD'S CREATIVE work. The Holy Spirit wants to make His home in us and He wants us to be at home in ourselves. Embodiment practices such as yoga and meditation, educational advances in Women's Health, and an inspired awareness of the intricacies of the Feminine Energy Cycle are powerful spiritual practices that women can embrace as a part of our holy journey.

Myth: Our bodies are cursed and cannot be trusted. Connecting with our bodies is a new age, witchcraft trick and forces us to abandon our faith.

It is devastating that when people set out to learn the wisdom of their body they often disconnect from God. The Spirit of God wants to meet us in our bodies; giving peace to tension, whispering truth into stillness, and blessing joyful expressions of dance, sex, and movement.

"God saw everything He had made, and behold, it was

very good and He validated it completely." (Genesis
1:31 AMP)

When God created man and woman in His image and
likeness, He said they were very good and validated them
completely. For centuries the body has been excluded from
any reference to the "spiritual self" that is being renewed.
However, in Colossians, the "spiritual self" Paul references is
connected to the human image of God from Genesis 1.

"Put on the new self who is being continually renewed in
true knowledge in the image of Him who created the new
self." (Colossians 3:10 AMP)

We are being renewed in wholeness - heart, mind, and
body together.

Many evangelical faith backgrounds operate from the
assumption that we shouldn't trust our bodies. They believe
the body is cursed and the Holy Spirit is only interested in
renewing our hearts and minds. Phrases like, "the wisdom of
the body," cause many to cringe and question.

The clearest declaration against this belief is the incarna-
tion. Jesus took on a human body and in His resurrection,
He was raised with that body fully intact. He invites us to
move with Him toward the same resurrected wholeness.

The Greatest Commandment also speaks of this wholeness. We are called "to love the Lord our God with our whole
self." How can we honor this Greatest Commandment if we
are not only absent from our body but also cursing her?

Our bodies, alongside the groans of all creation, are
longing for healing in wholeness. The more we understand

the language of our bodies and the movements she is making, the better we can partner with her and with all creation in the restoration that God is enacting.

May we know how fully we are loved, despite our mistakes, despite our humanity, or even, dare I suggest, BECAUSE of our humanity. May our practice of embodiment enable us to join our voices with our Creator that we are "VERY. GOOD."

—SARA ROBBERT
HOLY TRINITY CHURCH | CHICAGO, ILLINOIS

18

A TIME TO ROAR!

BY MS. ANGELA ENGLISH

"IF I WERE KING OF THE FFFFORRRESTTTT!"

Just like that, we're transported. There we are watching the cowardly lion sing his famous declaration song. Big curly haired lion. If only he had the courage. If only he had the strength. He could be king of the forest.

Truth is, he had all of those things already. Can I tell you, many of us are just like that. We're walking through life as cowardly lions unaware of our strength, and unaware of the courage we already have inside of us.

If you could, what would you say to that lion? What would you tell him? Is this what you need to tell yourself? It's really a matter of identity.

Our identity is in Christ. Knowing who Christ is and accepting who we are in Him, this is the key. We are the righteousness of Christ. We are more than conquerors; and we can do all things through the Christ who strengthens us. This is who we are as followers of the living God. This is you.

Today, walk in the truth of the word. Walk in the truth of

who you are. You are courageous and bold!! It's time to ROAR!!

The wicked flee when no man pursues, but the righteous are bold as a lion! (Proverbs 28:1)

—Ms. Angela English
Global Fire Church | Murfreesboro, Tennessee

19

INTENTIONALITY

BY AMIE ROGERS

EVERYTHING AS WE KNOW IT, HAS BEEN BREATHED INTO existence intentionally by God. From the very beginning of creation, every word spoken was done so with great purpose.

"In the beginning God created the heavens and the earth...
Then God said, "Let there be light" and there was light."
(Genesis 1:1-3 NKJV)

Throughout Genesis chapter one, we read about the purpose that was spoken over creation. In the creation of man, God made us in His image. "..."Let Us make man in Our image, in Our likeness..." (Genesis 1:26 NIV)

David even shares on the intricacies of our formation in Psalms.

"For You created my inmost being; You knit me together in my mother's womb...all the days ordained for me were

written in your book before one of them came to be."
(Psalms 139:13-16 NIV)

Every single thing the Lord has done and will do is
always drenched in intentionality. He is purposeful in everything He says to us while in our quiet time with Him. When
our lives are surrendered in Him, we begin to take on His
traits of Love and out of that Love for Him; intentionality is
birthed.

The revelation we receive in our relationship with God
only manifests out of the intentional time we set aside to
spend with Him. In turn, it manifests into every interaction
we have daily. Some interactions will be a fleeting moment
in time whereas others will be long-lasting relationships;
each requiring intentional effort.

When we look at the relationship between Naomi and
Ruth, we see two widowed women. Back in that time,
widows were ignored and poverty-stricken because they
weren't allowed to own anything. When their husbands
died, so did their identity. Yet, they stepped into their
purpose in the most unfavorable circumstances because of
an intentional decision. Naomi returning to her homeland
and Ruth clinging to Naomi declaring she was not returning
home. She couldn't go back to where she came from because
she heard of God's goodness and wanted more. Ruth had
now intentionally linked her identity with Naomi. "Don't
urge me to leave you or to turn back from you...Your people
will be my people and your God my God" Ruth 1:16 (NIV).
These two heart-broken women, intentionally clinging to
each other, moved forward.

In the midst of our most unfavorable circumstances, it

may not feel or appear like it, but we are still walking in our purpose. The Lord gives us connections to others that a lot of times don't make sense, but you do sense "these are my people". When you get connected, your heart is opened to harvest things you never would have before. Our intentional time with the Lord will open our hearts to intentionally connect and interact with people that will create lasting, meaningful relationships.

Father, we thank you for your intentionality towards us and we ask you to help us be just as intentional with everyone we know and meet. Amen.

—AMIE ROGERS
RawandRealMinistries.com | PEORIA, ILLINOIS

20

TITUS 3:5

BY KEILY J. DENNY

THE LORD SHOWED ME A VISION OF A FOOT THAT WAS IN BAD need of a pedicure. It had layers and layers of dry, cracked, dead skin all around the sides and bottom. The skin looked dry and ashy. It had calluses on it. It was REALLY in bad shape.

The vision changed to the foot soaking in water. Someone came and lifted the foot out of the water and tried to scrub the dead skin off of the sole of the foot but, the skin was too tough and needed to soak a while longer so, they put the foot back into the water.

I don't know how long the foot soaked in the water or how many times it was taken out and put back in. Eventually, the skin softened and it was easier for the person doing the pedicure to scrape and rub the dead skin off. The foot was restored with all of the dead skin removed -- it was good looking and smooth to the touch.

The Lord explained to me that this is the condition of our hearts and our thinking, including our faith and our relationship with Him. The Word of God, the Blood of Jesus, hearing the Word of God preached, our prayers, and our fasting washes away the calluses in layers a little bit at a time, until eventually, our hearts, our minds, and our faith are smooth and washed clean. This metamorphosis causes us to become a beacon that draws others to God, who lives inside of us.

This is a process; it does not happen overnight. There is a chipping away of the old that reveals the new. This is how we become a new creation in Christ. This is how we are born again in the Spirit by Jesus, the Living Water. He washes us clean as snow and makes us whole — body, mind, and soul. The longer we "soak" in Him, the more He can reveal to us for His glory. We receive what we believe. Faith grows with a smooth heart. A smooth heart comes with a soothed mind. A soothed mind comes when scales are removed from the eyes. Scales are removed from the eyes as the spiritual wax is cleaned out from the ears. All of this happens from a divine appointment from the Holy Spirit. He is the only one who doles out invitations to meet Jesus.

"...He saved us through the washing of regeneration and renewal of the Holy Spirit..." (Titus 3:5 Darby)

—KEILY J. DENNY
SHEKINAH REIGN | NASHVILLE, TENNESSEE

21

DO YOU KNOW WHAT IT FEELS LIKE?

BY SHARI A. SMITH

Do you know what it feels like to be a woman?

Do you know what it feels like to be a woman in a world where we are told to submit? To be told from the time we're old enough to speak that we must be silent because it was our rebellious nature that damned humanity?

Do you know what it feels like to be a woman in a world where we are told that our bodies are instruments of sin? To be told that a glimpse of our flesh is enough to cause our brothers to fall into sin?

Do you know what it feels like to be a woman in a world where we are told that our holiness demands the loss of agency over our own bodies?

Do you know what it feels like to be a woman in a world where we are told that man exists to mediate between us and the Lord?

Because, it is implied, that we are too inherently sinful to directly approach the throne of God.

We are told how to dress to avoid leading others into sin.

And if someone should sin because of our wardrobe choices, God help us.

We are told the limitations of what we can do with our bodies. And if we dare stray, God help us.

We are told the thoughts to think and the beliefs to hold. Even our inner voices and how we view ourselves are given to us by our churches, pastors, teachers.

Can we stop building a gospel around protecting the egos and fragile sexuality of men?

Can we stop building a gospel that is centered around controlling and manipulating women and girls everywhere?

Can we have a break to just be human? To live, breathe, and move in freedom.

Answering to no one but God Himself?

—SHARI A. SMITH
EZER RISING | WASHINGTON

22

KNOW WHO YOU ARE & WHOSE YOU ARE

BY CHERYL BENDIX

WHEN I WAS PREGNANT WITH OUR THIRD CHILD, THE STATE IN which we lived at the time required a blood test to determine whether the fetus would have down syndrome or spina bifida. I had the test and the result indicated our baby could have down syndrome. My doctor recommended I terminate the pregnancy. I told him that was not ever going to be an option for us and that led to us needing to undergo further genetic testing and an amniocentesis.

These additional tests proved in fact that our daughter was perfectly normal. Afterward, I learned the test only had a 50% accuracy rate, which is quite alarming. I remember being upset that my doctor would be so quick to recommend an abortion and wondering how many young women who didn't really know themselves would agree to it without fully investigating their options. For us, raising a child with any sort of special need was ok; they would be loved no matter what. This decision has given me a passion for the unborn, and for women who are faced with making these tough choices in life.

It is imperative that we know who we are in Christ, that we are so confident in our identity, we fully understand that we truly are who He says we are, that when the waves come crashing, we aren't swayed. When the world doesn't agree with our stance on something, it's okay because we are confident in our identity. Once we are confident in our identity, we need to be confident in our calling; what God has purposed us to do while on this earth. We can waste years of our lives chasing a dream that doesn't line up with what God has purposed for us to do, even if it lines up with our giftings.

We see so many people today confused about who they are. Some are confused about their gender. Others are confused about their callings, which leads to confusion about the callings of others. I love the story in John 21:15-33 where Jesus tells Peter how by his death he would glorify God and he (Peter) asks about John. Jesus tells Peter it isn't Peter's business, but God's alone what another's future holds. We cannot covet what another has, no matter if it is possessions, anointing, giftings, calling or position.

It is up to the Lord how he dispenses but together as the Body of Christ we work together to accomplish His will. So let's not get caught up in who is doing what, but how we are using the giftings and abilities God has given us to accomplish His purpose. What is it to me if another has a loftier position here on earth or a more recognized ministry? What is it to me if they have more followers on social media? What is it to me if they have a bigger house or drive a nicer car? There is a reason the Lord ended the 10 Commandments with a warning about coveting. He understands how it will lead us down a path of discouragement and destruction, derailing us from our calling. Let us stay the course, knowing who we are and Whose we are!

—CHERYL BENDIX
CHRISTIAN FAITH FELLOWSHIP | PONDER, TEXAS

23

JOY EVERY DAY

BY TAWNYA JOHNSON

"The Lord is my strength, my shield from every danger. I trust in him with all my heart. He helps me, and my heart is filled with joy. I burst out in songs of thanksgiving." (Psalm 28:7 NLT)

JOY COMES FROM THE INSIDE OF WHO WE ARE TO THE OUTSIDE. It is deep in our hearts. Joy is like a tree planted inside of us and it's roots go deep into our being. The only way we can have that kind of joy is through Jesus. In Psalm 28:7 qualities are described and then joy is planted. We need Jesus' strength, His shield and His help. He is faithful and never leaves us. He is the same God now just like when He spoke to Moses. God told Moses the He will be with him (Moses) and won't fail him. (Deuteronomy 31:8) We can put our trust in Him. He has our back. When we release our control over our lives to Him, joy can be filled deep in our hearts.

How can we have that kind of joy every day? Every time the sun rises, it is a new day with a new opportunity to have fresh joy in our lives. Take time with Jesus. He wants a relationship with you. He wants to hear your voice talking to Him and you listening to Him as well. I challenge you to be aware of Jesus being in your day. It doesn't have to be a long time, it can even be in your car during the commute to work. Take note of what blessing you have from Jesus. Notice the slightest feeling of direction, comfort, love and contentment. Those are bits of Jesus showing up in your life. Have joy that He is perusing you and wants to be with you.

When your hearts are poured out to Him, He will fill you back up with joy. It will not matter what situations go on around you. You have joy from Jesus who saved you, fights for you, loves you and cares about you. Grab onto Jesus and be filled with His lasting joy.

—Tawnya Johnson
King's Grace Fellowship | Junction City, Oregon

24

THE LORD WILL FIGHT FOR YOU

BY JEANNE ALLEN

"The Lord will fight for you, and you have only to be silent." (Exodus 14:14)

"For the Lord your God is He who goes with you to fight for you against your enemies, to give you the victory." (Deuteronomy 20:4)

THERE ARE DAYS WHEN THE FIGHT IN MY LIFE, IN THE AREA I live, in the US, in the world, overwhelms me. When all the encouraging words fall into an empty well and echo back at me as trite phrases with little or no meaning. I lose perspective that today is just reflective of today and not tomorrow, or the day after, or the month or year after. I allow the microscopic problems to become the cloak I wear, and I no longer see the Father's glory, His steadfastness, His rock.

And on one of those days, I read the two verses above. It brought me back to a vision My God had given me several years earlier. I was on the battlefield, fully covered in metal armor, helmet on my head in a battle-ready stance, but the sword I held was a long toothpick. And then I raised my eyes to the heavens and saw God's angel warriors, tall broad men on horseback, menacing in size and presence, with full long swords drawn and ready to fight my enemy. It was a humbling vision of me trying to deal with my life challenges, and I accepted the grace-filled offer to have these warriors fight for me.

When I read these verses above and surrender my challenges, my conflicts, my worries to My God, I am reminded of His greatness, His faithfulness, His redemption across my life. I am reminded that we ARE in a fight, and we need to not lose sight of this; that the evil one is always looking at ways to make us stumble and fall so that in our weakness, we'll just cave in to him, to his lies, to the old ways of coping he taught us.

I am reminded that that the evil one is defeated, fighting from a chained position, ranting and raving at me to get my attention. But he is chained, and My God did that for me. And as I turn each moment over to My God, giving Him praise for who He is, acknowledging my status as Daughter, my Kingdom inheritance, I feel His strength ebb back into me, His peace seep into my bones.

And I rest, knowing, trusting, believing that He is fighting for me, will win the battle for me, and will call it my victory because He loves me that much.

Father, thank you for loving me so much that you will fight my battles. Thank you that you eagerly await my request to do so.

Thank you that you WANT me complete dependence; that it's not a burden but a delight. Holy Spirit, do your work in me; teach me. In Jesus' name, amen.

—JEANNE ALLEN
FC GRACE | WARRENTON, VIRGINIA

25

WHO'S YOUR DADDY?

BY TERRI FAIR

WHO'S YOUR DADDY? GOOD QUESTION. I DIDN'T HAVE A perfect father and let's face it...who has! While my earthly father wasn't perfect, he was a formidable figure; While he was kind and compassionate, I knew not to disregard his instructions. Heads would roll! My father was strong, a hard worker. He worked two jobs to provide for us.

Many have not had good kind fathers. When earthly fathers wound, it creates a barrier to draw close to our perfect heavenly father. Even when trusting Jesus as Savior and Lord, the father wound remains until we can learn that He has the best in mind for us and trust Him to heal us.

The warrior walker must have confidence in Father God, that He is good. Knowing to Whom you belong will give you the building blocks, the solid foundation to stand as a warrior. He is who He says He is and He will do what He said He will do! You must know that about Papa God no matter how untrustworthy your earthly father was. When we receive Jesus, He makes all things new. It may be instant or it may be a process. Our job is to believe!

Who's your Daddy? Read this passage out loud from 2 Samuel 22. Read it and read it and read it and read it again until your spirit sores with the joy of knowing your Daddy is good!

My Daddy is my rock, my fortress and my savior: My Daddy is my rock in whom I find protection. Daddy is my shield, the power that saves me and my place of safety. My Daddy is my refuge, my savior, the one who saves me from violence. My Daddy rewarded me for doing right. Daddy restored me because of my innocence.

Daddy you are my lamp. You light up my darkness. In your strength, I can crush an army; With you I can scale any wall.

Daddy's way is perfect. All His promises prove true. For who is my Daddy except the Lord? Who, but my Daddy is a solid rock? Daddy is a strong fortress and He makes my way perfect. He makes me as surefooted as a deer...He trains my hands for battle;

You strengthen my arm,...You give me your shield of victory, Your help has made me great, You keep my feet from slipping. You have armed me with strength!

Who's your daddy? *This is your daddy.*

SCRIPTURES TO PONDER:

"The Lord is like a Father to His children, tender and compassionate to those who fear him." (Psalm 103:13)

"The same way a loving father feels toward his children, thats but a sample of Your tender feelings toward us." (Psalm 103:13 TPT)

—TERRI FAIR
LIFE CHURCH | SALEM, OREGON

26

WARRING WOMEN ARISE!

BY KATIE GIBSON

"The earth shook beneath Your feet; the heavens filled with clouds before the Presence of the God of Sinai. The sacred mountain shook at the sight of the face of Israel's God. You, O God, sent the reviving rain upon Your weary inheritance, showers of blessing to refresh it. So there Your people settled. And in Your kindness You provided the poor with abundance. God Almighty declares the Word of the Gospel with power, and the WARRING WOMEN OF ZION deliver its message: 'The conquering legions have themselves been conquered. Look at them flee!' Now Zion's women are left to gather the spoils." (Psalm 68:8-12 TPT)

I HEARD THE VOICE OF THE LORD SAYING:

"It is time for you warring women of Zion to arise and take your place! Open your mouths and decree and declare the

Word of the Lord to your families, community, regions, and the nations!

Do not hold back at establishing justice, righteousness, and freedom right where you are!

You have been given this land as your inheritance and THE TIME TO CLAIM IT IS NOW!

You are appointed warriors! Warriors advance and take possession of the land and the spoils that are before them! They do not draw back in the fear that leads to destruction.

You have been given the strongest and most victorious weapons of the Lord, the greatest being the Sword of the Lord, to conquer the darkest of enemies.

Claim your families! Claim the lost around you! Claim that which has been rightfully given to you!

Your specially designed roles have great power in bringing the Kingdom of Heaven to earth here and now!

Press in and press forward to breakthrough!!!"

"She sets her heart upon a nation and takes it as her own, carrying it within her. She labors there to plant the living vines." (Proverbs 31:16 TPT)

We as women have been given the gift of the nurturing

spirit of God. This gift exemplifies the Father's loving heart to our children and those around us. It is this very gift that compels us to take up our children, a nation, a promise... and cultivate them into fruit-bearing trees of life that we can bring to God as an offering of praise.

Deep within the nurturing spirit of God is also a fierce force that drives us to guard these pearls with our very lives. You need not worry about any opposing force; you need only rest in the victory of God and the power of His Word. It is this sacred and holy place that, when cultivated properly, becomes the seedbed for your inheritance, blessing, vision, direction, promises, provision, restoration, revival, and every other thing you need.

Rise up in this reality of rest with Him and fix your gaze upon His face. Raise the war-cry of abundant victory and fruit; then charge forth and plunder the enemy's camp as the Commander of Angel Armies drives them out!

—KATIE GIBSON
GIBSONS GO GLOBAL | FORT WORTH, TEXAS

27

WHO ARE THEY ANYWAY?

BY JESSICA KALASHNIKOV

WHO SAID YOU COULDN'T? WHO SAID YOU SHOULDN'T WHO said you wouldn't? Who are they anyway? The Lord says:

"I am with you, I will guide you, I approve you."

Many times we are scanning the room wondering what "they" will think, we are writing our blog wondering if they will approve, we are living our lives questioning our actions our motives comparing ourselves to that person, those people, who are they? This is what the Lord says:

"You belong to Me, and I have appointed you for a time such as this."

If we are living to please someone else we will never truly live. There will always be people who disagree or don't like your flavor that's why we need so many delicious flavors! You must release your scent or you'll lose your fragrance. One of the most satisfying permissions you'll ever receive is permission to be you. And I hope this will stir in you a niggling thought that won't relent until you've said yes to ALL of you, you are not too much and you are not lacking, come alive. This world will be missing that most satisfying last piece of the puzzle if you're not showing up in your sphere of influence.

—JESSICA KALASHNIKOV
CHRIST'S CENTER | EUGENE, OREGON

28

DAUGHTERS OF EVE

BY ELIZABETH WALKER

I LOOKED INTO THE MIRROR AND I REJECTED WHAT I SAW. NOT just my physical features, but everything in, around, and about me. I tried to reason with myself, that it wasn't my fault that I felt this way, and it was "OK" to think like this given my current life situations. But that excuse fell flat the second that it came from my mouth. The Holy Spirit reminded me of Genesis chapter 3, and an all too familiar Bible story, but this time I saw it in a new way.

Genesis 3 says, 'The serpent was the shrewdest of all the wild animals the Lord God had made. One day he asked the woman, "Did God really say you must not eat the fruit from any of the trees in the garden?" "Of course we may eat the fruit from the trees in the garden," the woman replied. "It's only the fruit from the tree in the middle of the garden that we are not allowed to eat. God said, 'You must not eat it or even touch it; if you do, you will die" "You wont die!" the serpent replied to the woman. "God knows that your eyes will be opened as soon as you eat it, and you will be like

God, knowing both good and evil." The woman was convinced. She saw that the tree was beautiful and it's fruit looked delicious, and she wanted the wisdom it would give her. So she took some of the fruit and ate it.' Did your heart drop on the same sentence that mine did? "The woman was convinced."

I'd like to think that I would protest and debate a bit farther before I accepted the serpent's advice, but the reality is... I never have. I've never questioned whether or not I needed to be more. A thousand slogans about being "Perfectly Imperfect", "Who You Are", or "Bea-U-tiful", and I cannot really remove that feeling of less. That feeling that seems to start at a young age, yet rears its serpent head in our teens, bites into us and keeps us poisoned throughout our adult life. Eve was not immune to this feeling. Eve wanted to be more. Why did the serpent choose Eve as his initial target? Maybe because he knew her weakness. He knew, being the shrewd animal that he is, that he could plant a seed of questioning in Eve's mind and she would water it with her own doubts until it bloomed into the biggest, ugliest, weed in the garden. For God created women to take what was given to her and nurture it. Satan uses that beautiful ability and womanly nature to his advantage. She was convinced. Eat this fruit, and she would finally be whole. Lose 10lbs, and she would finally be noticed. Get this promotion, and she would finally get respect. Get a whole new wardrobe, and she would finally be able to hold her own with the other women in her life. Get the guy, and she would finally feel complete.

What is your fruit? Now, not all fruit is bad, and in fact this fruit wasn't all bad. It was Good... and Evil. It was good where it belonged, in the parameters it was meant to stay in. On the tree in the middle of the garden as a reminder of how only God makes us whole. It becomes bad when we devour it ourselves and look inwardly (and outwardly) to make us complete. Putting on make-up, dressing up, working hard, and staying healthy are not bad things. In fact, they are mostly good. God created us to thrive, to desire beauty and strength, and to be able to do unimaginable and amazing things. The Father gave each of us an undeniable and beautiful purpose and calling, each one as valuable as the others. We are daughters of Eve of Eden. The name Eve literally means to give life. We are called to bring life, in whatever shape, form, or way, that God designed us for, in whatever place He set us. We were created as a missing piece needed to complete a masterpiece, not a "someday masterpiece" just waiting for completion. For too long, we have let ourselves and our sisters, believe the poison that the serpent injected into Eve many years ago. I don't have an instant cure to this snakebite, but I know the One who does. His name is Jesus. I want to see a reflection of Him every time I look into a mirror.

"But you are a chosen race, a royal priesthood, a holy nation, a people for His own possession, that you may proclaim the excellencies of Him who called you out of darkness into His marvelous light." (1 Peter 2:9)

—Elizabeth Walker
King's Grace Fellowship | Junction City, Oregon

29

DISCOVERING THE SECRET PLACE

BY JESSICA KLAUSING

In 2016, Phil Wickham wrote a song devoted to realizing that God is our sanctuary. The song is called The Secret Place, and it speaks to the strength and beauty that comes from finding the place where we are free with the Father; a place where Father and child are eagerly searching to bless the heart of the other. A private place of communion with Him, where we find fulfillment and refreshment. However, the part that has reverberated over and over in my head, is our call to action in the secret place.

> "I'm running to the secret place where you are, I'll sing to you of all the ways you stole my heart."
> —Phil Wickham, *"The Secret Place"*

In my own experience, each person's secret place is suited to them. My secret place looks different from that of my friend. While mine is in a grass pasture, with a forest, a stream to the left, and mountains before me; my friend's is in the middle of a wildflower field. I'm standing on a blanket in the middle of the pasture surrounded by books, while she is joyously dancing in circles. Although differing in appearance from one another; the actions inside are one in the same. We are freely, and joyously singing directly to, and sometimes with, God. You see, our secret place is not a physical place. Rather, it is a spiritual place designed for our fears and our joys, a place where we sing to God about the beauty He provides. It is where we find the life we seek and the joy we crave. When we run into our secret place, we run directly into the presence of God, where we are able to obtain all that we are needing and seeking.

"I'll sing to you of all the ways you stole my heart."

The best biblical picture we see of this concept, is the life of King David through his Psalm writings. King David had no problem telling God all the things he wished God would change, of the pain and exile he was tired of suffering. But in each of those laments, in each of those songs, David finishes by singing of the love of God. Psalm 13:6 (TPT) is the perfect example. He finishes it by saying:

"I will sing my song of joy to you, the Most High, for in all of this you have strengthened my soul. My enemies say that I have no Savior but I know that I have one in you!"

My challenge for myself, my friends, and for you is to do as Wickham alludes to in his song, to move boldly into that special space of one-on-one communion with God. It may feel strange as you learn to move into this place, but the more you work on seeking communion with Him, the easier it becomes to find yourself in that secret place; and to sing to Him of the ways He has truly stolen your heart.

—Jessica Klausing
New Life Christian Church & World Outreach |
Columbia City, Indiana

30

GOD IS NOT BREAKING YOU

BY JENNIFER MARTIN

WE OFTENTIMES SAY, "GOD IS BREAKING ME." ESPECIALLY when we go through really tough times. And I get it, because I've been there and sometimes it feels like I live there. It feels like you're breaking, being crushed, suffocating.

But I was shown what is actually happening to us in these times. The Bible says in Isaiah 64:8 - "But now, O LORD, You are our Father, We are the clay, and You our potter; And all of us are the work of Your hand." So our God is the great potter and we are the clay on the potter's wheel.

While a potter is shaping and forming his creation, at what point does he break it? Why would someone who is putting all their heart into this clay, actually get fed up, take it off the wheel, and break it? I can't imagine anyone would, and neither does our God.

What feels like breaking is the making! You think you're being crushed but you're actually being formed and molded. You think you're being suffocated but in reality you're being held by the potter's hands. You are exactly where you're supposed to be.

Don't jump off the wheel! Yield to His hands. Trust Him. And the entire time His eye is on you, making sure you form into the work He's imagined in His heart.

This process is precious to Him.

God is asking us to stop saying that we are broken. We are never broken, but in the process of becoming. We are being conformed into the image of his Son.

That's not breaking, *it's making!*

I could feel the deep sincerity of our Father as He shared His heart with me about this. He never does destructive acts to you or any of His children. It grieves Him when we use this term "breaking."

He is always at the potter's wheel, working on you, and when you're ready, He puts you in the fire. Not to burn you but to complete you fully. And nothing can ever break you, because He finished the work. It is done! And He has placed you into the fire of His Holy Spirit that seals you forever. And you're coming out shining!

—Jennifer Martin
Contagious Love International | Antioch, Tennessee

31

REDEFINING HELPMATE: THE WOMAN'S WARRIOR ETHOS

BY MARIJEAN SANDERS

EVER SINCE I WAS YOUNG, I'VE FELT A WARRIOR SPIRIT BEAT IN my soul. At the same time, the intensity of my nature craved solid edges to give shape and form to my energy. So when my conservative, bordering-on-fundamentalist authority figures told me, you exist to be a helpmate for your husband and family, I enthusiastically embraced the prescribed structure even though the associations I carried with the word – mostly jean jumpers and casserole dishes – didn't quite fit my personality.

Over the years, the jean jumper persona gave way to a sleek Instagram mama vibe, complete with shiny minivans and cute bootie-and-cardigan outfits, sanitized playdates, and expensive homeschool curriculums. But I couldn't keep up (or settle in) to any of that either. Even the joyful days when I caught little shallows of sanity in the eddies of chaos, I still felt like I was not only failing but also suffocating.

I knew this work wasn't without value, but where was it all going? As I moved through the world, trying to curate the perfect household, manage the perfect calendar, and bake the perfect pie, something in me felt strangled. Despite the frenzied motion, I sensed a certain stagnancy. I craved a forward force of movement that made the whirling vortex of wife-and-mama life feel like I was spinning my wheels.

Forever an etymology nerd, I did some research. I discovered that the word helpmate in Genesis 2 comes from the Hebrew phrase ezer kenegdo. The word ezer (translated help) is used twice to refer to women and several times to refer to military allies. It is also used 11 times to refer to the Spirit of God...as a warrior and rescuer of his people.

Take Deuteronomy 33:29: "Who is like you, a people saved by the LORD? He is your shield and helper and your glorious sword. Your enemies will cower before you..." That's not referring to washing up the dishes after a meal, is it? Or juggling the family calendar?

Ezer means warrior. It means strong rescuer. Savior, even.

And kenegdo? Whether shoulder to shoulder as battle-companions, or forward and flank, like pilots in formation, I discovered that the usage of kenegdo consistently connotes a meeting of equals, combining strength and strategy for an outcome of victory.

It finally dawned on me: The root of the problem is not that I am falling short. On the contrary, the standard isn't high enough! The full realization of my role is far more expansive than having time to apply makeup every morning (as if that ever happens!) and pack the most adorable, dinosaur-shaped snacks in my kiddos' boxed lunch. I was made for much more.

I say: raise the standard, warrior women. Cultivating a

specific visage of womanhood isn't the fullness of our purpose and experience. Let's wave the flag of power and creation, leaning into our roles as women of God, made in Her image to bring forth beauty and healing into a world that desperately needs our gifts.

—MariJean Sanders
North Manchester, Indiana

32

BIGGER DOORS OF DESTINY

BY SULA SKILES

Love encounters with the Lord transform the way we think about obeying Him. We move from unsuccessfully striving and feeling obligated by legalism, to adventurous, heavenly, love drenched encounters that cause us to race after His Voice. Jesus becomes our first love forever and we remain giddy at His every move... Longing to be with Him, our Bridegroom King, and serving Him at all cost.

> "Loving me empowers you to obey my commands." (John 14:15 TPT)

I am one of the least qualified to do anything "big" for the Lord. I've lived a life of trauma, pain and a lot of sin... Childhood of sexual abuse, mental illness, abortions, suicide attempts, addiction, sex trafficking and more. Everything changed when I fully surrendered to the Lord. Previously, I was partially obedient, but still leading my own life. I rededicated my life to Jesus, meaning that my life was no longer my own. As a result, He has opened Doors of Destiny and His signs, wonders and miracles have become a part of my everyday life.

I've been asked many times, "How do such big opportunities come to you?" My answer is probably not the answer most want to hear... Radical Obedience. I don't think the Lord is looking for the "qualified," but for obedient yielded lovers. Jesus set the perfect example for us when He said, "I only do the works that I see the Father doing, for the Son does the same works as his Father" (John 5:19-20 TPT). What are the things that prevent you from obeying God? Jesus is asking His bride to rid herself of her idols. He wants to open bigger opportunities to you, but you must cut out anything that prevents you from obeying His voice. Allow Jesus to heal the places of hurt and purify the places of sin. Remove the little foxes that destroy the vine of intimacy with Jesus (Song of Songs 2:15). The bible says that "obedience is better than sacrifice" in 1 Samuel 15:22-23.

> "So this is why we abandon everything morally impure and all forms of wicked conduct. Instead, with a sensitive spirit we absorb God's Word, which has been implanted within our nature, for the Word of Life has power to continually deliver us. Don't just listen to the Word of Truth and not respond to it, for that is the essence of self-deception. So always let his Word become like poetry written and fulfilled by your life!" (James 1:21-22 TPT)

As we learn to love His Word, hungry to encounter Him, He opens doors for us that no man could ever open. As long as you remain obedient to the Lord, you are NOT going to miss what He has for you. Trust Him fully and you won't have to figure it out on your own, or position yourself through motives or manipulation to obtain success. At the end of it all, Jesus is our reward. He is the Door. He is the Way.

—Sula Skiles
SulaSkiles.com | Destin, Florida

33

NO LONGER HIDDEN

BY MARISA LOTHER

"This is why I remind you to fan into flames the spiritual gift God gave you when I laid my hands on you. For God has not given us a spirit of fear and timidity, but of power, love, and self-discipline. So never be ashamed to tell others about our Lord." (2 Timothy 1:6-8 NLT)

GROWING UP, I WAS ALWAYS KNOWN AS "THE SHY KID." THE quiet, reserved, and observant one. This was who I was for so long that I started accepting it as my identity. I grew accustomed to a lifestyle of less than. I believed this timidity was already rooted so deep within me that I would be forced to deal with it my whole life.

Because of this, I never thought I could be a leader or speaker. I settled with hiding in the shadows, staying silent and neglecting the gifts God placed within me. This opened a gateway for the enemy to come in and feed lies into my mind. These lies gave rise to insecurity and confusion at a young age, building up over time and creating an unhealthy perception of my life.

Just recently, amidst an essential season in my life, I came across this scripture and realized that God has not created me to be hidden. He does not want to keep me locked in a box, restricting my growth. I am a child of God and therefore have been called to a life of boldness, power, and breaking the box.

He wants the very best for me, including the freedom to be who He has created me to be and do what He has called me to do. This year God spoke to me clearer than I have ever heard to start sharing my poetry and encouraging words to the world. This revelation was huge for me. I had never felt so pulled by the Holy Spirit to take a leap of faith and step out of my comfort zone.

It was debatably the hardest and scariest decision I've ever made but looking back at all that God has done in my life following this act of obedience, I know undoubtedly that it was worth it.

Since starting my poetry page, I have grown tremendously and met such amazing, passionate people. I cannot even imagine where I would be if I had not obeyed. If I had given up this crazy idea, let fear win, and chose the easy, comfortable route instead.

God has called us to be bold both in our everyday lives and in the precious gifts He has given us. We each play a part in His master plan. We each have a story to tell, ideas to share, and things to create.

When it comes time for your moment, don't let worry get in the way. You and I were not made for this fearful life, we have been called to something so much greater. Come out of hiding and shine bright for the King.

—Marisa Lother
Awakened Garden | Pensacola, Florida

34

THE BURNING ONES

BY MONICA RAMEY

THE BATTLE OVER YOU AND YOUR SOUND HAS BEEN EVER SO long. It happens all around you. Resistance.

You, whose voice has been resisted, stifled and denied. You are no stranger to the storm.

But I see a company of burning ones coming on the scene. They're rising up out of the ashes and coming straight out of the wilderness.

No longer walking in rejection, reproach or seeking the approval of men, but baptized in fire and endorsed by heaven.

These fiery ones won't be received by some. Their moves will not be understood or received by the ones quenching and controlling spiritual climates, or by ones bound in religious tradition.

Those operating like Saul won't have the understanding or the capacity to receive it and will come against it. Their moves and words will be too fiery, and not understood by the carnal mind. (1 Corinthians 2:14 NKJV)

These women of God will be solid in their identity and they will not be moved. They will not be looking for the permission of men, but will be led by the Spirit of God. (Romans 8:14 NKJV)

Those that come into contact with these daughters and receive them will catch the fire from heaven themselves. Moves of the Spirit will start spreading and begin to burn all over the map!

Arise, shine;
For your light has come!
And the glory of the Lord is risen upon you.
For behold, the darkness shall cover the earth,
And deep darkness the people;
But the Lord will arise over you
And His glory will be seen upon you.
The Gentiles shall come to your light,
And kings to the brightness of your rising.
(Isaiah 60 1:11)

Arise burning ones, ARISE AND SHINE!!!

—MONICA RAMEY
MONICA RAMEY MINISTRIES | PORT CHARLOTTE, FLORIDA

35

AM I ENOUGH?

BY PATTIE ANNE

Every now and then, a certain song, movie, or incident will cause a wave of nostalgia to flood my memories, sweeping me back to certain times in my life. I sometimes sit in awe of the decisions I've made and the profound regret and grief that resulted. The dreams I had as a young girl seemed to evaporate. My testimony turned out to be, "I wish I was someone else, living with someone else, residing somewhere else, and doing something else." Too often I felt unhappy and unfulfilled.

Yet, I had been a believer in my savior, Jesus, since I was young. I should have been fulfilled and satisfied in Him. Why wasn't I? Why did peace and happiness seem to evade me? All those unwise decisions had turned into one disappointment after another. Since I, myself, was to blame, I always felt "trapped" with no way out.

All began to turn around for me when I became part of a group of women who met regularly to seek the Lord and minister to one another. We discovered several jewels of revelation that changed everything! First, for me, was the astounding truth regarding spiritual adultery! What is it? For me, it was always being dissatisfied with what the Lord had provided and upset with Him for not changing anything.

It's so easy to sing, "Jesus, you're all I need," and then whine to Him about what I don't have. He tells me to be thankful and rejoice in all things, yet, I struggled to recognize good in anything. The Apostle Paul had learned to be content in all circumstances, whether having much or little. Yet, nothing seemed to be enough for me.

The Lord says He'll make everyone "free indeed" if they stay in His word and seek His face. We're to have no other gods before Him. Suddenly, I realized I had been looking to my family and situations for fulfillment. When I sought purpose, contentment, love, or joy in people or things, I was guilty of spiritual adultery! Jesus longed to meet my needs. He desired to be my first love. Oh, the wonderful relief in repentance and submitting to Him. His love and acceptance bring such serenity, driving out all guilt and regrets. No more striving to please, afraid to fail. The only thing that matters is falling in love with Him over and over each day. Me and my hurts are no longer in the picture - genuine freedom!

I'm learning to sincerely delight in Him, soaking in His presence and love each morning. Jesus is becoming my only source. Miraculously, I see everyone and everything around me differently – through eyes of love. Jesus changes everything! There is no end to His joy and fulfillment! My testimony has become, "Yes, Lord, you are more than enough!"

—PATTIE ANNE

BREAKING BREAD WITH PATTIE ANNE | SALEM, OREGON

36

LIVING MY BEST LIFE

BY CHRISTINA BERGMAN

"I'm energized every time I enter your heavenly sanctuary to seek more of your power and drink in more of your glory. For your tender mercies mean more to me than life itself. How I love and praise you, God!" (Psalms 63:2-3 TPT)

I ALWAYS SMILE WHEN A HEAR THE PHRASE, "LIVING MY BEST life (lmbl)." I suppose it's from all the different things that make people momentarily happy. How many women really are living life to the fullest? Are things like yoga, coffee and Target the epitome living our best life?

I want to encourage you to not get short changed in life. Whenever you feel lifeless, disconnected and alone, go straight to our Heavenly Father. He is life! Just like we cultivate relationships with our friends by working out together, enjoying long conversations over coffee and Target runs, we have to be intentional in cultivating our most important life-giving relationship with Jesus. In Psalms 63, David can't stop talking about God and His goodness. We can have that amazing life and relationship with Christ too through prayer, worship and mediation of God's truth, love and goodness. It's every day, all day. Our time with Him is so energizing and changes our life focus. We begin to feel alive, connected and desiring for even more of His glorious presence and goodness.

Heavenly Father, I have felt lifeless, disconnected and alone so many times. I've short changed myself by getting my focus on the wrong things. Today, I shift my focus back on You. I choose to live my best life in You and through You alone. In Jesus Name, Amen.

—CHRISTINA BERGMAN
NEW LIFE CHRISTIAN CHURCH & WORLD OUTREACH |
WARSAW, INDIANA

37

I WEAR MY CROWN

BY APOSTLE KARIN LOMBARD

ANOTHER DAY DAWNING. I STRETCH OUT MY ARM, AND REACH for..... my Crown. Right here, next to me, I see it's reflections playing on the wall. My mind fills with the rays of Joy, it's a new day. I pull it closer, feel the weight of its jewels rest in my hands. Confident I sit up, and throw my head back joyfully. A smile unfolds across my face as I lift up my Crown, and place it, firmly on my head.

Yes, I am the head, not the tail, and I am crowned in His Righteousness. I am a Woman who is virtuous, pure, and my price is far above those of rubies. Oh how gracious the gift He placed in me, and generous He was. Creating me according to His purposes and plans. Plans to prosper me, and give me hope, a future. I rise now in my place for I am courageous, and brave. He's made me in His image.

I go into this day, knowing that I am valuable, I have a voice, and I have wings. There are no voices that will tell me otherwise, as I know my Father's voice. It's full of power, and majesty. I dress myself in His authority, and kindness looks good on me. Tastefully I choose to walk forward victoriously. He crowned me as a victor, here is no victim. Those challenges on my journey are stepping stones, and I look back at my beautiful path. All along He's been holding my hand. He leads where I follow.

I encounter those who appose, and know that my words will be constructive and true. My tongue speaks in kindness. I'm a gatekeeper, and use my sword wisely, it compliments my crown. This crown of gold, surely purified, and fire proofed, as I rise above, beyond reproach.

My day fills with praise. I walk tall, reminded of the glory I carry. A glimpse of my reflection in the mirror, I smile and give her permission to be kind to herself. In the distance, my sister walking. We have many differences, yet we have so much in common, and my heart says, be kind to her. Be kind to the stranger, be kind to the one who walks in doubt of who you are, and where you are going. Your way might not be clear to them, as you are still pathing that unseen way. Continue, and do not stop, your crown carries the honor needed to complete your journey.

The lovingkindness and mercy is in my crown. I am grateful for being chosen to wear it with wisdom, and peace. Every morning I rise, and hear my father's voice, the greatest gentleman I've ever known. "My darling, you can do anything you want, as long as you do it like a lady." What he said: "Hold fast what you have, so that no one will take your crown." (Isaiah 28:5)

—Apostle Karin Lombard
Karin Lombard Ministries | Omaha, Nebraska

38

SO BEAUTIFUL

BY ALEXA ROSE DUNNIGAN

"Every part of you is so beautiful, my darling. Perfect your beauty without flaw within." (Song of Songs 4:7 TPT)

Two wooden beams and the highest price paid. One body bore the world's weight of sin to become the bridge of forgiveness that reconciled family and bought back His bride. An unfathomable ransom. A precious price. One man defeated all death and took upon the greatest suffering that hung to sing a melody over us:

"I LOVE YOU. I DESIRE TO BE WITH YOU. I AM YOUR BELOVED AND YOU ARE MINE."

His naked body clothed us. He became shame so that we could shine. His crown of thorns redeemed the jewels for ours. The holes in His hands gifted us a ring of eternal promise. His death raised us to life.

These two wooden beams declare "I came TO GET HER.

I came so that we would be together forever."

Jesus sees nothing more beautiful or more radiant than His bride. We were His joy set before Him to endure the suffering of the cross. Beloved and beautiful, He invites us to see ourselves as He sees us.

Only He will cause every dark, dead and lied to place within us to become a beautiful bouquet of flowers. If it's not beautiful yet, He's not finished. In these hidden places, we discover Him as our resting place and our soul's true love. As we gaze upon Him, His beauty perfects ours.

It is a most courageous act to believe in the holy truth and goodness of our beauty. Our beauty matters to Him.

Pause in His presence and whisper these words with Him:

Beautiful Jesus, thank you for the cross. Thank you that you came to get me. I desire just as David desired to be with you, "That I may dwell in the house of the Lord all the days of my life, to behold the beauty of the Lord, and to inquire in His temple." (Psalm 27:4)

I do, Lord. I lift my eyes to gaze upon your beauty and to be with you. I invite you into every place I have judged myself as unworthy or anything less than truly beautiful. Jesus, I chose to let you love me. Will you come author fresh faith and show me what you see? Teach me to put my faith in your beauty and to receive every truth of how you see me — altogether beautiful.

—Alexa Rose Dunnigan
UPPERROOM | Dallas, Texas

39

ENTER JESUS

BY MICHELL LYNN BURTON

Jesus said to her, "You don't have to wait any longer, the Anointed One is here speaking with you—I am the One you're looking for." (John 4:26 TPT)

Have you ever read the story about the woman at the well, and wondered "Where are all of her friends?" Most women during that time traveled to the well in the early morning, the coolest part of the day. But not her. She went at noon. By herself. When Jesus met her there, they were alone.

Her story always resonates deep within my soul – broken marriages, broken relationships, a broken heart. I'm left to wonder what her thoughts were when she walked to the well and back home each day. Were they filled with regrets, self-loathing, hurtful words or angry retorts she would never get to speak? Even now living with a man who wasn't her husband, it must have been the loneliest time of her life.

She walks alone.

She stands alone.

She strives alone.

It saddens me to think that she was not surrounded by friends – her sisters, her tribe.

Enter Jesus....

In a simple exchange about life, living water, worship and salvation, this woman experiences the Messiah. A welcome breath of fresh air. A taste of freedom. A touch from God. When she returns to her town, she returns a different woman. Her situation hasn't changed, her relationships haven't changed. She doesn't care about her past or present circumstances. Her heart is the one that has been transformed.

This transformation compelled her to reach out to others, even when they had turned their back on her. Her goal was clear: to tell as many people about Jesus. Nothing else mattered.

In a world where our lives can be fast-paced and self-centered, let's be women compelled to tell others about Jesus. Let's be women who love others regardless of their past or present circumstances. Let's be women that surround women at the well of their lives and offer them a chance at a new life. Jesus went out of His way for this ONE woman. Shouldn't we do the same?

—MICHELL LYNN BURTON
CHAMPION LIFE CENTRE | SPRING, TEXAS

40

FINISHED

BY FRANKIE HARNESS

BEFORE ANYTHING IS MANUFACTURED AND SENT OUT TO fulfill its purpose, it is first planned out, made, and then tested. It is completely finished and proven to be fully capable of accomplishing its purpose before it ever hits the hands of the consumer. A product is always finished before it ever starts. In the same way, God has manufactured you. There had to have been a plan finished for Him to send you to start. Before He ever sent you to this world, He planned out every detail of who you would be and what you would need to impact this world for His glory. He placed inside of you unique characteristics that others may not have and at times you may not like but those things may be the very tool you need to be effective at leading people to Christ. Once He was finished planning you out and piecing you together, you were then finished and He sent you to this world to fulfill a specific purpose. One made specifically for you.

Many times, we feel like we have to somehow earn a purpose or plan or that we have to be built before we are given a plan or purpose. The truth is, we were created in Christ Jesus to fulfill a plan He created long ago for us (Ephesians 2:10). Psalms 139 talks about how our steps were already planned our for us, everyday of our life was laid out before a single one had passed. We are not here by accident, and we are not designed to fail. We have been tested and approved.

But the key to living life to our fullest potential is relying on the One who made us and knows us the best. According to 2 Timothy 3:16-17 " All Scripture is given by inspiration of God, and is profitable for doctrine, for reproof, for correction, for instruction in righteousness, that the man of God may be complete, thoroughly equipped for every good work." We must continually be in God's word for instruction and guidance in living out this preplanned life. God's word is our manual to find out our best features, how to protect ourselves, and how to live out our full potential. Jesus Christ is our warranty. We go to Him when we need repaired or updated. The Holy Spirit is our 24 hour tech support. He is available at anytime to help answer questions, give understanding, and bring clarity.

By realizing you have a finished purpose, you are able to walk with confidence that each day has a purpose and you are fully equipped to complete it.

Read 1 Corinthians 2:6-12

—Frankie Harness
New Life Christian Church & World Outreach |
Warsaw, Indiana

FOR MORE INFORMATION

To access more information about the project, to be a contributor for future devotionals, or to place a discounted bulk order of this book, visit:

TALLPINEBOOKS.COM

instagram.com/tallpinebooks

NOTES

Publisher's Note

1. Tammy   Devaraj | https://www.facebook.com/photo.php?fbid=
   10219057197675193&set=a.1699057070599&type=3&theater

Made in the USA
San Bernardino, CA
20 December 2019